How to Write a Book AND Get it Published

Debbie Hardy

How to Write a Book AND Get it Published

by Debbie Hardy
Author, Speaker, and The Queen of Resilience

Published by
Stepping Through Life
12210 Brighton Road, # 452
Henderson, CO 80640

ISBN-13: 978-0-9908390-0-2
ISBN-10:0 990839001

Cover photo by Debbie Hardy (Yep, those are my books on my sheet!)

Back cover photo by my cinematographer son
Brian D. Harmon with
Bully Curious Productions

And thanks to my daughter-in-love Sarah Harmon for her help with cover formatting.

For more information on writing, publishing, or the author, visit: www.DebbieHardy.com.

This book and its author present no guarantee that following the advice herein will guarantee you a bestselling book.

But give it your best shot. You never know . . .

Table of Contents

Here we go!..9

1. Get an idea...11

2. Learn all you can...13

3. Attend writers' conferences. 16

4. Develop friendships. 19

5. Join a writers' group...........................22

6. Determine your audience. 25

7. Read every day. 28

8. Write what you know. 31

9. Write what you're passionate about.
....34

10. Format your manuscript before you start writing..37

11. Puke your book out...........................40

12. Write a query or a proposal. 43

13. Rewrite your entire manuscript...46

14. Read your manuscript out loud....49

15. Grow thick skin...................................52

16. Have your manuscript critiqued and edited...55
17. Build a platform.................................58
18. Rewrite and have your manuscript critiqued again..60
19. Get a copy of a Writer's Market Guide...63
20. Submit ONLY to agents or publishers who work in your genre...66
21. Check websites for submission guidelines and current contact information...69
22. Keep accurate records of what you send to whom. 72
23. Wait...74
24. Keep building your platform. 76
25. While you're waiting, keep writing. 79
26. Don't take rejection personally. ...82
27. Keep a record of suggestions included in your rejections, if offered. 85

28. Wait again. 88
29. When an agent wants to represent you, they'll send a contract. 91
30. Be nice to your agent. 94
31. Your agent might be working on a deal. 96
32. Wait some more. 99
33. Consider self-publishing, AKA independent publishing. 101
34. You will need to buy your own books. 104
35. Don't hold out for an advance. ... 107
36. Read a contract before you sign it. 110
37. Research royalties offered and compare to the rest of the market.... 113
38. Wait a little longer. 116
39. Marketing is up to you, not the publisher. 118
40. Send a copy of your book when you request an interview. 121

41. Hire a publicist. 124
42. Practice being interviewed. 127
43. Find an image consultant. 130
44. Research your interviewer. 133
45. Let your contacts (your platform) know about any interviews you have. 136
46. Don't expect to be paid for being on TV or radio shows. 138
47. Write thank-you notes to the producer and the host. 141
48. Keep a detailed record of your appearances and contacts....................144
49. Don't quit your day job. 147
50. Write every day. 150
Have at it! 153
Appendix 1 154
Endnotes...156
About the Author 157

Here we go!

Many people with the urge to write a book have no idea what is involved. They've probably told amusing stories at parties and had someone say they should write them down.

Maybe that's you. And now you're ready to write and publish your book. It's not easy, but it *is* possible with the knowledge here and stick-to-it-iveness.

Having written a book will put you in an exclusive group, as not everyone can make that claim.

Tom Clancy said, "Success is a finished book, a stack of pages each of which is filled with words. If you reach that point, you have won a victory over yourself no less impressive than sailing single-handed around the world." (1) What an accomplishment!

But writing the book is only the first part of the process.

Here's a list of steps in the writing and publishing process, with an explanation of each one.

This is not an exhaustive roadmap, but it gives you an overview of what's involved. These steps are not necessarily in chronological order and you might work on more than one at a time.

Whether you want to publish for the world to read, write your grandmother's story for your cousins, or share memories and dreams with your grandchildren, don't give up. You never know when your book might become the next bestseller. And you don't want to quit right before that happens.

So, let's get started!

1. Get an idea.

Write whatever you feel like, maybe similar to what someone else has written but from a different point of view. You don't need to create a strange world or a new genre of fiction. Just use your imagination and think up something original.

The Book of Ecclesiastes, says, "There is nothing new under the sun." (Ecclesiastes 1:9) Unfortunately, that's true. Just about every book you read or movie you watch is an old story reworked to seem original.

"West Side Story" is "Romeo and Juliet" updated with music added. "Cinderella" has so many variations that the only difference seems to be the wardrobe. "Robin Hood" movies boast several big-name stars and varying stories but always the same goals for the title character. And don't get me started on the hundreds of adaptations of Charles Dickens's "A Christmas Carol."

Come up with something like yet unlike anything you've read or seen. Maybe you can set your story in a different location or era. Or combine two stories, like "A Tale of Two Cities" meets "Green Eggs and Ham."

Your nonfiction book could provide a new way for people to handle an old problem. Or maybe you experienced something very few people face or handled a common dilemma in a surprising but successful way.

Just make it new. Make it you. No one can talk like you, write like you, or come up with your ideas.

Have fun!

2. Learn all you can.

This book is a good start for you to learn about writing and publishing. We'll look at the basics, but there are a lot of things that we won't have time to delve into.

When you set out to be a writer, you are embarking on a new career. This is an industry, just like telecommunications, retail sales, or manufacturing. You wouldn't dream of changing careers without learning how to do the new job, whether you study ahead of time or get on-the-job training.

The more you learn about writing and publishing, the better equipped and calmer you'll be with the process. Anything can be easier if you know what to expect.

There's more to writing than you ever thought possible, even if you did well in high school English classes. Knowing how to construct sentences and paragraphs puts you ahead of the pack. The ability to string those together into a cohesive novel or nonfiction book without preaching lands you in an elite group, but only if you know what you're doing.

Look for books, videos, magazines, online or in-person training about writing, especially if they explain an aspect of it you need to learn. One may teach character development, another how to write an instruction manual. You can't cover everything in one class, so plan on spending hours – yes, hours! – honing your craft.

When I teach at writers' conferences, the director will usually let faculty members block out time to attend others' workshops they are interested in. Many of these folks have been writing for years and have lots of books published. Yet they realize there is so much more to know and will keep learning.

If multi-published authors, agents, and editors are continually looking for training, maybe a new author would do well to keep learning. That's why I still attend classes!

3. Attend writers' conferences.

Conferences provide workshops on various steps in the process, like the craft of writing, getting an agent or a publisher, and marketing your book.

I teach at both the Colorado and the Greater Philadelphia Christian Writers' Conferences. Each of these has over 100 workshops to choose from because there's so much to learn. And the workshops vary every year.

Many writers' conferences will tell you that you can meet agents, editors, publishers, publicists, and authors. But that usually just means that you'll be in the same room with them, not actually meeting *with* them.

Instead, look for conferences that offer one-on-one appointments with faculty members. This gives you a chance to get feedback and pitch your story to someone who can help you get it sold and published.

When someone you've met with requests that you send a proposal or manuscript, ***send it right away!*** About 70% of conferees will feel their work isn't good enough and won't submit when requested. Sending yours will increase your chances of getting accepted and published.

If someone requests your work, they like it the way it is. Send it now and they might offer you a contract. They may not, but you won't know unless you take the risk.

One of my writer friends waited 3½ months to send her requested manuscript, only to learn that the agent had signed a similar novel just the week before. Another reworked her manuscript so much that the agent didn't like it any more.

Whether or not someone asks for your manuscript, keep going to writers' conferences. There is always more to learn and the industry is constantly changing. Not only are books and publishing methods fluctuating, but the way they're marketed and sold keeps morphing.

Never stop learning.

4. Develop friendships.

Most writing is done alone and many writers are introverts. It may not be easy for you to make friends, so take every opportunity to step out and be around others, especially those in the same business.

A writers' conference is a great place to meet those farther along in the publishing process. You can rub elbows with authors, agents, and publishers, folks you probably would never meet otherwise.

I have a lot of "once-a-year friends" whom I see only at annual conferences. We stay in contact during the year through social media or email. And when we get together, it's like we haven't been apart.

People enjoy working with folks they like, so try to be likable. Don't be phony, just nice. Not everyone will work with your type of writing, so don't get upset if they don't offer you a contract. That would be like getting upset because your mechanic doesn't sell groceries.

This is an industry of relationships, so create and maintain as many as you can.

A word of warning – just because you've connected with someone at a conference or online doesn't mean that you're automatically best friends. These conferees and faculty members may be willing to help you on your publishing journey, but they don't want you to show up on their front doorstep.

That actually happened to one editor. The over-eager writer now has a restraining order and a reputation that will probably keep her from ever getting published. Don't sabotage your future by obsessing over one person.

Share yourself with others. That's the way to be a friend.

5. Join a writers' group.

We write more words than our readers want to read. If we don't tighten up our writing and get rid of the excess, no one will want to slog through. But we tend to be very defensive about our writing. Every word is from deep inside and expresses what we want to say, so it's only natural to be protective of them.

That's where a critique group can help. These are writers who assist each other to improve their manuscripts and encourage one another to keep writing. Listening to suggestions and editing your manuscript can make it better and easier to read.

It's like going to a support group. You encourage each other, praise accomplishments, and push one another to achieve more than you could by yourself.

Just to clarify, there is a huge difference between criticism and critique. Criticism says, "This is bad." That doesn't help. Critique says, "This can be better and here's how." That can improve your work.

One of my friends, a fabulous author, joined a group of writers in her genre. However, they were interested more in their own books than in helping anyone else. After trying to be accepted and listening to only criticism, she left that group and joined one that was more supportive.

Your group needs to meet often enough to make a difference. My writers' group met once a month when I first joined. Sharing only a few pages each time meant that it would be years before we'd get through a manuscript. When we increased our meetings to once a week, we wrote more, learned more, and completed more books.

Your family and friends don't understand what it takes to write a book, but your writers' group members do. They can empathize when you get a rejection and cheer when an agent requests your manuscript.

Find a group that will help you and commit to attending it regularly.

6. Determine your audience.

Don't write for "everyone." Try to focus on who you're talking to.

Every book, movie, and TV show has a message, a point it's trying to communicate to its readers or viewers.

It's obvious in nonfiction books what the message is – usually the subtitle will tell you. But even fiction has a point to the story. "Star Wars" teaches us that humans are smarter than machines. "Harry Potter" shows that good will triumph over evil. "Oliver Twist" proves that your life can improve and that others can help.

You have a message that you want to get across to someone or to a group of people. Figure out who needs your message and write to them. This may be a particular age group or people who are interested in a subject or going through a similar circumstance.

It helps to have an image of your audience. A male friend of mine edited a magazine for teen girls. Since he had never been a teen girl, he cut a picture of one out of a magazine and taped it to his computer screen. Then, he wrote to that girl and got his message out to those who needed it.

While I was writing *Stepping Through Cancer: A Guide for the Journey*, a friend was undergoing cancer treatment. So I wrote my book to his caregiver wife Judy, and it reads like a conversation on the couch with her.

Don't make your audience too narrow, like "35-year-old accountants who've been out of work in the Denver area for three years," unless you have a message specifically for that group of people. But if you do, don't expect to sell many books.

Decide who needs to hear what you have to say and direct it to them. If you write well enough, they'll pass your message to others and increase your audience.

That's how bestsellers happen.

7. Read every day.

Too many people feel that reading is a luxury or something unimportant. When I was in high school English, reading a book was required. However, when my dad saw me reading, he would tell me to quit wasting time and do something productive. I didn't start reading for pleasure until years later.

Reading can help you write better. Read anything you can get your hands on: books, magazines, internet articles, blogs, or whatever. This will not only expand your vocabulary, but also improve your grammar and writing ability.

You can see how the work is crafted and absorb ideas for your own writing. Also, you'll find errors in others' writing and learn not to make the same mistakes.

One friend enjoyed romance novels but didn't read them much. She decided to write a romance different from all the rest. When her book was published, it wasn't what romance readers were accustomed to and the book didn't sell.

A good writer will read one hour a day. If writing is your career, consider that hour part of your job. It's required work, so you don't have to justify it.

Keep a book handy, in your purse, in the car, or on your nightstand. When you have a few minutes, grab that book and get to work.

When you have several books going, don't worry about trying to keep all the different stories straight. Just back up a page or two and reread what you covered last. That will refresh your memory and get you right back into the story.

If you don't like a book, you don't have to complete it. Toss it and pick up one you like. I've read some books that were so bad, I refused to donate them to a thrift store and risk having someone else read them. Instead, I recycled them with the trash.

Read for fun!

8. Write what you know.

Your brain is an amazing computer, full of memories, ideas, and imagination. Using what you already know is much easier than having to research what you don't.

My first book was for cancer caregivers. I was a caregiver when my husband was in a serious car accident and then again when he was diagnosed with cancer. Since I wrote from my experience and memories, the book just flowed out.

Set your novel in the town where you live or grew up and have your characters in jobs that you've had. It'll be much easier for you to make it believable. And knowledgeable readers will notice and appreciate that.

An author in my writers' group set her cowboy romance in Kansas until she realized that she didn't know what kind of terrain, weather, or vegetation was there. She was facing a lot of research to make her book accurate, so she relocated her story to her home state of Colorado. It was much easier to just write without worrying about making mistakes her readers would catch.

Another author set his story in a city that he had visited. Since he wasn't familiar with the roads there, he used a city map to plot his car chase scene. And I as a reader had to use a map to follow the story. Needless to say, his book wasn't too popular.

If you write something foreign to you, readers may catch errors and discount your knowledge, ability, and status as a writer. They could write reviews online that will damage your credibility and your book sales, so stick with what you know.

With a nonfiction book, readers expect more than a quick gloss-over of information they already know. Choose a topic about which you know more than the average person and can be an expert. Provide some value in your book, something that can improve lives.

9. Write what you're passionate about.

Writing and publishing a book can take years, and if you're not passionate about the subject, you'll tire of it long before the process is completed.

My first book took only three months to write, so I didn't have time to get bored with it. However, having it critiqued, rewritten, edited, and revised took much longer, so that seemed to drag on.

Once it was typeset by the publisher, I had to proofread it again and again, and it became overwhelming. We went through 11 revisions and I had to read it every time to check for errors. If I weren't passionate about helping cancer caregivers, I would've given up.

I've started several books and never wrote Chapter Two. The ideas weren't bad and it was easy to outline the rest of the book. But I wasn't really excited about the topics, so I didn't finish them. Maybe one day I will, but not today.

Your passion will get you through the tedium of rewriting, rereading, proofing, and marketing the same thing over and over. And you'll be answering the same questions again and again when interviewed about it on radio and TV.

You can also be passionate about fiction. Some authors get so caught up in their characters and story line that they will write for hours without noticing the clock. You may need to take a break every once in a while to prepare a meal or tuck the kids in bed. But if you can hardly wait to get back to writing, you have the fire.

If you're not excited about your book, don't expect anyone else to be. Stick with what animates you, what keeps you awake at night, what you cry or pound the table over, and others may become enthused about it as well.

Your passion will come out through your words. And your readers can tell when you’ve poured your heart and soul into your work and they’ll be more engrossed in your book.

10. Format your manuscript before you start writing.

There is a standard way to format your manuscript. You don't want to be rejected because you didn't format correctly.

This may sound a little nit-picky, but there's a very good reason to follow standard formatting.

Publishers, editors, and agents can get hundreds of submissions a week. If every writer used a different font, margins, and size of lettering, it would take longer to peruse all of them.

It's like getting job applications that are all free-form and having to look for the info you need. A fill-in form makes it easier for a hiring manager to find the info they're looking for.

Whether you write fiction, nonfiction, or magazine articles, always, always,

always format your document this way:

- Font Times New Roman, size 12
- Margins 1" all around
- Line spacing double
- Indent first line 0.5"
- No added line between paragraphs

It's easier and less problematic if you format BEFORE you start to type. One friend would type a chapter, then reformat the document before taking it to writers' group. Many times, she got so accustomed to seeing the wrong font that she forgot to reformat.

Also, grammar rules have changed and we no longer double-space at the end of a sentence. In fact, if you do, your manuscript could be rejected. Not keeping up with current grammar is a sign of an amateur.

Just a quick note – If you publish your own book, you can use whatever font you want. You may be tempted to use "pretty" letters, but they don't always convert the way they look in your manuscript.

Also, your lines and indents still need to be standard or the publishing and typesetting conversion software may have problems.

Be sure to order a copy of your book to approve it before you offer it for sale.

11. Puke your book out.

I know this sounds gross, but puking your book out is exactly what you need to do. When you physically "toss your cookies," you keep puking until everything is out, and then you clean it up. Same thing with writing. Get it all out from inside you, and then clean it up.

No book was ever published before the author wrote it. Isn't that profound? But it's true. In order for your book to be published, you have to write it.

Many writers get so busy editing, rewriting, and perfecting Chapter One that they never get to Chapter Two. Just figure out where you want to go with your book and set out to get there.

Some writers are plotters – they outline the book to create a roadmap and then flesh it out.

Others are “pantsers” – they write by the seat of their pants, just letting words flow.

Plotting will help you stay on track and end up where you intended.

“Pantsing” makes it harder to stick with the original story, since your characters can take you wherever they want and your writing can wander.

Once your book is written, it can then be edited and published. So just write it.

The best way to write is the BIC method: Butt In Chair. If you don’t schedule time to sit down and write every day, you probably won’t follow through.

Start with a goal of 300 words a day. That’s about one page double-spaced. When you achieve that for several days, increase your goal. Many authors with multiple books write several hours a day, even while holding down a day job. You can too.

Just sit down and write.

12. Write a query or a proposal.

If you want your book published through an agent or an editor, you'll need to prepare a document they can read to get to know you and your book without having to wade through your entire manuscript.

Nonfiction books require a proposal, which includes a synopsis and sample chapters. The book doesn't need to be completed, but state in the proposal how long you anticipate it'll take and how many words you'll end up with.

Novels (fiction) must be completed before you pitch an agent or an editor. Your query will include a synopsis of the entire story. Since they will be selling your book, they need to know how it ends, not just that there is a "surprise ending."

Proposals and queries have a strict format. If you're creative and write them however you want, you'll probably be ignored. Agents and editors can get dozens of these a day, so they need a standard setup. If you can't follow directions for the initial contact with them, they know you won't cooperate with other requests they have.

Get a book, attend a class, or search online to learn how to write your proposal. The opening is like a letter, so it's single-spaced. You can double-space between paragraphs, but not the whole thing and definitely not your synopsis.

Sample chapters are standard manuscript format:

- Font Times New Roman, size 12
- Margins 1" all around
- Line spacing double
- Indent first line 0.5"
- No added line between paragraphs

Your proposal will likely be between five and 40 pages long.
A query is much shorter – more like a job application. These have strict guidelines, so check the agent's or publisher's website and give them what they're looking for.

Address your proposal or query to the correct individual, and be sure to spell their name correctly. They're people just like you, and will toss a generic letter or one with errors.

13. Rewrite your entire manuscript.

Writing can be a done in a stream of consciousness, just letting your brain wander. Your readers don't want to cut through all that fat to get to the meat of the story. And you'd probably end up with a longer book than anyone wants to read.

According to author Stephen King, your second draft equals your first draft minus 10%. (2) That means that if you wrote 100,000 words, you need to edit out 10,000 of them. I once wrote a nonfiction book and ended up with 64,000 words. It needed to be 35,000-55,000, so I worked hard and got it to 54,300 words. That's 9,700 of my "darlings" that I killed off the page.

Here are some things to look for when editing:

- Adverbs, usually ending in "-ly," slow down the story. Instead of saying, "He walked slowly," say, "He ambled" or "He strolled." Same idea, fewer words. And every word counts.
- Remove one unnecessary word from each sentence.
- Sometimes we use two prepositions when one will work, like "He stepped out onto the balcony." The balcony is outside, so in order to get onto the balcony, he *had* to step out. Revise it to, "He stepped onto the balcony."
- Conversation tags, like "he said" or "she said." If only two people are talking, just remind us every so often whose turn it is. Other than that, we can follow the dialogue.
- Read your story out loud to catch extra or duplicated words.

- If you find your tongue tripping over a passage as you read aloud, rewrite so it sounds more natural.
- You may find two words that say the same thing and eliminate one of them. Instead of saying, "There was only one exception," say, "There was one exception."

If you've ever said something that you wish you hadn't, this is your chance to pre-edit it in writing. Remove those words before you regret them.

14. Read your manuscript out loud.

Reading your book out loud may sound strange or feel awkward, but, believe it or not, you can easily catch errors or sloppy phrases.

When you read, "He was good boy," your brain fills in the missing "a" but your mouth will notice its absence. When you find yourself tripping over a sentence or a phrase, that's a signal to rework it to make it sound more natural.

Another issue that writers face is repeating words. Reading aloud helps your ears notice that you've used the word "house" a lot, for example. Replace one or more with a synonym.

With few exceptions, my writers' group won't allow an author to read her own work. A writer will read what they intended to say, while someone else will read exactly what's on the page. Since you can't sit next to everyone who reads your book and explain what you meant, your work must stand on its own.

You can also hear your "voice" when you speak aloud. If it's not the way you would talk in normal conversation, or if the words have too many syllables for the message you're sending, rewrite it.

Your characters might have an accent or a different way of talking, but the story, the narration, is *your* voice. Keep that "voice" consistent and grammatically correct.

Write your characters' dialects when you introduce them, but don't belabor it. Too many "goin'"s or "gotta"s or other methods of showing their way of speaking slow down your readers. There are times when I'll quit reading one character's spoken words when it's too hard to understand or makes me read it out loud. That's too much work.

Some writers dictate a book into a recorder and then transcribe, so it really sounds like they're talking. Your readers want to feel that you're sitting with them, telling them what you want them to hear.

That's the second-best compliment a writer can receive – that your readers felt like you were talking just to them.

(The number-one compliment is that something you wrote changed their life. Not very frequent with fiction, but very rewarding for nonfiction.)

15. Grow thick skin.

Rejection is a way of life for writers. You will be rejected, no matter how great a writer you are. Of the hundreds of authors I know, only one was accepted by the first publisher she contacted. That normally doesn't happen.

When you pitch (or submit) your book to an agent or a publisher, you are one of hundreds of authors looking to get published. They can't print every book or they'd go bankrupt. They need to pick the ones they feel would sell best and make them money.

Think of it like dating. You meet someone and think you have something that could develop into a relationship. But chances are you won't marry the first person you date. You may reject them or they could reject you. Either way, it wasn't a good fit. And that's okay. There are others.

When you receive a rejection, tell yourself that the person who will love your manuscript is at a different address. You just need to find them.

If an agent, editor, or publisher asks you to send them your query, proposal, or manuscript, they like their first impression. But that doesn't mean that they'll still want to sign you after they've scrutinized your work.

An agent requested my proposal, which meant he was interested in my book. A few months later, I received an email response from him. All he did was hit Reply and attach a document named "Reject.doc." I didn't have to read the attachment to know what it said.

Eventually, I found an agent who loved my work and we've had a great relationship. And we now have a publishing contract.

It can happen for you too. Just keep that thick skin in the meantime.

16. Have your manuscript critiqued and edited.

Even bestselling authors use "fresh eyes" to read their manuscripts and catch errors, repetitive words, or other things readers may not like. In his book, "On Writing," Stephen King shares a manuscript he wrote and shows how it needed editing. [3] If a multi-million-book-selling author still gets his manuscripts critiqued and edited, how can we think we write better than he does?

After attending my first writers' group and listening to their comments about how to change my "divinely-inspired-by-God" book (or so I thought), I was devastated! I cried all the way home and put my manuscript away, swearing never to work on it again.

A few days later, I decided to prove them wrong and incorporated every suggestion. But those ideas actually made it better and easier to read. And I've attended that writers' group ever since.

But just because someone suggests a change doesn't mean that you need to go with it. We all have our own "voice," the way we talk, whether audibly or in print. Read your work out loud to be sure any changes still sound like you.

There are several stages in the process when your manuscript can be edited. You may need some input on your book idea from someone who can help focus your story or thoughts before you start writing.

At other times, an editor can point out awkward sections or places where your story drags. It's better to get feedback from an editor than a reader who buys your book and posts a negative review for all the world to see.

Think of it like ironing your clothes. They've been cleaned and are hanging in your closet, but when you put them on, those wrinkles keep you from looking your best. A little touchup can make all the difference between looking good and looking great.

Have someone help you "iron out the wrinkles" in your writing.

17. Build a platform.

Your platform is made up of people who will likely buy your book. They will also tell others about it, so the larger your platform, the more books you could sell.

Your platform will include your contacts and all your social media. Don't forget your family, friends, coworkers, and church or club members. Everyone who knows you is part of your platform, so the more folks who know *and like* you, the better.

Publishers use this info to decide whose manuscripts to accept. If you have 300 in your platform and another author has 10,000 followers of their blog, chances are the other person will get the contract.

Don't wait for your book to come out to start building your platform. New friends won't appreciate it if, the day you meet them, you try to sell them a book. Establish relationships early, so they'll recognize your name and be excited when your book launches.

The idea is to "create buzz," or get people talking about you. This is where your platform comes in handy. You announce your book to them, and they tell all their friends about it. Word-of-mouth can be very effective – and cheap – advertising.

This is not a one-time accomplishment. Keep building your platform, even after your book is out. You'll need to sell your next book, so increase your readership now.

18. Rewrite and have your manuscript critiqued again.

The first draft of a book is usually wordier than it needs to be. And if your grammar is bad, it can get in the way of your story.

You want readers to love your work, so give it to critical folks for their reaction before even thinking about publishing. And don't become defensive when they tell you what they'd like to see changed.

These are readers, just like those you hope will buy your book and tell others about it. If you can make your book something that readers want, you're more likely to sell it.

You may want to hire a freelance editor. This will cost you, but it will be worth it in the long run.

Most editors charge one to two cents a word. That means that editing a 50,000-word nonfiction book can run $1,000. And an 80,000-word novel could cost $1,600 to edit. That may seem steep, but what would it cost you if people bought your book, found mistakes in it, and posted reviews telling others not to buy it? It could reduce your sales to zero.

Some editors charge by the hour instead of by the word. If your grammar is excellent, this can save money. You could have them edit the first part of your book, then you apply their suggestions to the rest of the manuscript. This will save the cost of editing the entire book.

Editing your manuscript is like cleaning your house. There comes a time when you decide that it's as good as it's going to be. You may find things later that you wish you had done differently, but don't worry about it.

Do the best you can and let it go. Just be sure it *is* your best!

19. Get a copy of a Writer's Market Guide.

The Writer's Market Guide provides information on agents, editors, publishers, and publications in the general market. The Christian Writer's Market Guide gives the same for the Christian market, which usually means for sale in Christian bookstores.

Some agents and publishers are crossover, meaning they sell to both the general market and the Christian market. These could appear in either or both guides.

You may find other market guides for children's books, young adult books, or poetry. Use the one for your genre and study it thoroughly. You could find these in your local library instead of buying them. But since they may be considered reference books, you might have to use them at the library.

The information in these guides includes names of agents, publishers, and periodicals with contact numbers and addresses. They will also give URLs so you can check websites for the most current information and target audience info.

Read all the data provided. Most will tell you what genres they want, how much they pay, timelines for production, and answers to many questions you may have.

There is so much info here that you could be overwhelmed. When I read my first market guides, I created a spreadsheet to list all the agents and publishers who *might* be interested in my book. Columns were labeled Name, Type (Agent/Publisher), Address, TN, Email, Website, and Comments.

I highlighted cells in green to note positive points and things to beware in pink (red was too dark). Then, instead of thumbing through 600 pages of paper books, I could just look at my list to make my decisions.

Use the Writer's Market Guide as a map. You don't need to read the entire map, only the part that points out where you want to go.

20. Submit ONLY to agents or publishers who work in your genre.

Just as there are different stores to buy different products, there are agents and publishers for different genres. These professionals specialize in the types of books they handle.

You wouldn't think of going to a hardware store for vegetables, so don't approach the wrong agent to pitch your book. If you've written sci-fi, don't submit to someone who deals with romance. And if it's a Bible study, someone known for children's books can't help you.

Address your letter to a person, not to a company. If you send something To Whom It May Concern, that's the same as getting mail at home addressed to Occupant. And they'll do the same thing with your letter that you would do with that Occupant envelope.

Agents work on selling your manuscript to publishers, but you don't pay them. Their "pay" is a portion of your royalties, the profit you make on each book sold. (More on agents later.)

Many folks will write a book and send it to a publisher without having it edited or critiqued. Publishers don't want to waste time on bad writing or someone who isn't serious about their craft. As a result, some only accept submissions from an agent.

If you have an agent, he or she has already taken the first steps in assuring that yours is a well-written manuscript. The publisher knows that your book will require less editing. They would be more likely to offer you a contract.

Also, agents have a reputation for the type of work they represent. When your agent submits your manuscript, the publisher is aware of the sort of work that agent is known for. That will give you a better chance of being accepted and published.

21. Check websites for submission guidelines and current contact information.

The Writer's Guide goes to print months before it's released, so some info may have changed.

Don't assume just because you have a publisher's email address that it's correct. After you've decided where to submit, check their website for the latest info. It will also give you the name of the appropriate contact.

Folks in the publishing industry are always moving around, changing companies. That doesn't mean they're bad at their jobs. It just means that someone else offered them a better position, pay, or opportunity or one company bought another. The acquisitions editor who accepted your first book may not be with the same publisher for your second.

When in doubt, call the company to verify. They would appreciate that you took the time and effort to send to the right person and not take the shotgun approach.

Some want you to submit online. Others want an email with attachments. Very few want paper copies. Whatever they request, provide them with it.

I once made the mistake of submitting incorrectly to an editor who is also a friend. He had requested a last-minute magazine article, so I obliged. I wrote a brilliant piece, attached it to an email, and sent it.

Within seconds (literally!), I got a reply telling me in no uncertain terms that if I had checked their website for submission guidelines, I would have known that they don't accept attachments. Not following the rules got me rejected before I even started.

If you want to be a rebel and do things your way, prepare to publish on your own. Agents and publishers want authors who will cooperate with them.

Bottom line: Read what the agent and publisher want and how they want it, then do it their way. It'll increase your chances of acceptance.

22. Keep accurate records of what you send to whom.

Some publishers will allow simultaneous submissions. You can send your manuscript to more than one at a time, as long as you tell all of them that you've done it. You needn't say who else got the manuscript, just that others are reading the same thing.

When someone accepts your MS and offers you a contract, let all the others know. They may be pushing your work through the process, and they won't appreciate that you let them waste their time when they had no chance of publishing it.

Others will require that you only submit to one company at a time. Each submission could go through several editorial boards before the publisher offers a contract. They don't want to waste all that time on something if the author is not committed to working with them exclusively.

If you meet someone at a writers' conference and they ask you to submit, they may not be interested once they have time to really read it. They may have liked the concept, but didn't like how you developed it. You might receive a polite rejection from them, but, more often, you won't hear a word.

Wait two or three months after submitting, then send an email letting them know that you'll submit elsewhere unless you hear back from them. Give them a couple of weeks. Then assume they're not interested, and go ahead and submit elsewhere.

Create a spreadsheet to list all the places you submit. If not, you may resubmit to a place that already turned you down. And they'll remember you, so be accurate.

23. Wait.

Be patient.

That's easier said than done, but it's necessary. One of the most important things in the publishing process to learn is waiting.

It takes two to three months or maybe longer for an agent or a publisher to respond. Some won't respond at all. Don't be offended; that's the way it is.

Don't try to "hurry them up" by bombarding them with emails or phone calls. That will only aggravate them and probably get you a quick rejection.

When you enter into a contract with an agent or a publisher, you're also entering into a long-term relationship. If you come across as pushy or controlling, they probably won't want to have a relationship with you, and you will get yourself rejected.

There's a fine line between requesting a response and demanding one. I can't tell you where the line is, but you'll know when you've crossed it. The best way to avoid crossing the line is to stay as far away from it as possible.

Learn to wait. It will do you well.

24. Keep building your platform.

Remember, your platform consists of everyone who will likely buy your book and talk to others about it.

Don't be content with what you have. Always be looking for ways to increase your platform.

The more people you can get to talk about you and your book, the more books you'll sell. That's why even best-selling authors and actors will make commercials about a new book or movie and go on TV and radio to discuss it.

Try other forms of social media. Your target audience may be online, so go where they are.

Be positive so people want to connect with you. If on social media you're always posting something negative or political or trying to sell your book, you'll turn off more people than you'll attract.

Be consistent. When you establish a following (people who like what you have to say and how you say it), they know what to expect from you. They won't like being surprised if you write something totally out of character.

Ask for opinions or input. Things like "What's your favorite...?" or "Tell us about..." can get conversations going. When others add comments, you connect to their contacts and increase your platform.

Even though writing is a solitary endeavor, learn to break out of your shell and be around people. Become well-versed in the art of small talk. Then join clubs or associations where you can meet folks.

Don't hit them over the head with the fact that you're an author the moment you meet. That's like a salesman introducing himself and then trying to sell you something. You might as well wear a plaid jacket to announce your presence!

Let the fact that you're an author creep into the conversation. Believe it or not, that will raise others' opinion of you. Enjoy it!

25. While you're waiting, keep writing.

It can take months or years to get an agent or a publisher. If you do no writing until you land a contract, you'll probably never write another book.

While you're waiting, write something else. Keep a journal, start on your next book, post a blog, or write magazine articles or devotions.

When you start another book, outline how you want it to start, how you want it to end, and how you'll get there. Once you have the idea and the roadmap, do the BIC thing. Put your "Butt In Chair" and just write.

There are times when the second or third book an author has written gets published first. And once readers buy that book and like your writing, you can go back and pitch previous books to your publisher.

Create your story by stringing together a series of snapshots. Help your reader picture what's happening to draw them into your world. A short story can be easier just because it has fewer words, but it must still be complete.

When writing a magazine article, it's better to know which magazine you'll pitch. Check their word limit and write the article to fit. Or query them to see if they'd be interested in a piece on your topic, then write it after they send you a contract.

If your article gets published, you can get free advertising for your "upcoming book." At the end of articles, there's usually a little bio of the writer. You compose it yourself, so give the name of your book even before it's published. Then, mention that article in your query or proposal. A magazine can have a circulation of 25,000 or more, which increases your platform exponentially.

No matter what you decide to write, just write it. You have all these words inside of you waiting to get out, so set them free.

26. Don't take rejection personally.

I said it before: Rejection is a way of life for a writer. You pour your heart out on a page and offer it to someone you hope will love it as much as you do. Unfortunately, very seldom does the first person accept it.

Sometimes you'll get a response that your manuscript isn't what they're looking for. That doesn't mean you're a bad writer or that you have a lousy idea. It only means that *your manuscript isn't what they're looking for*. Nothing more than that.

You may submit to more than one at a time to increase your chance of acceptance. But it's like dating several people at once. It's best if you let them all know that there are others.

Many successful authors received dozens of rejections before publishing that bestseller. Jack Canfield and Mark Victor Hansen were rejected by over 100 publishers for "Chicken Soup for the Soul." That's only counting the ones who actually said no; others just ignored them. They went on to sell over *200 million* books in the series. Then they sold the Chicken Soup name for another $60 million!

Being ignored is a silent way of getting rejected. Just as you can't answer every email in your inbox, agents and editors can't either. If they take the time to respond with constructive criticism, be open to their ideas and keep submitting.

A rejection only means that the person who will love your manuscript is somewhere else. Your job is to look around for other prospects and find the right one.

Change your vocabulary. Instead of saying, "I got a rejection," say, "I got a response." That way, you weren't really rejected.

You just received a response. And now you're free to submit to someone else.

Go for it!

27. Keep a record of suggestions included in your rejections, if offered.

Most rejections are standard form letters, addressed to "Dear author" with generic "No, thank you" wording. Polite, but not personal. One of my rejections was only a Reply email with a document attached named "Reject.doc."

If someone sends a personal note with their response, thank them in writing. That editor or agent has no obligation to read everything you send, take the time to analyze it, and tell you what could make it better. You could develop a relationship and they might become your friend and ally.

Not every suggestion should be incorporated into your work. Others write differently and may want your writing to be just like theirs. Decide what will work for you and what to ignore.

It's like getting dressed for work and stopping at every house on the way to the bus to ask your neighbors what they think of your outfit. Each might have a different suggestion, but you can't remove your jacket AND leave it on. You have to decide which.

When you know what someone is looking for, you have a better idea what to write the next time. Maybe this manuscript doesn't fit the bill, but if you wrote a story for a different age group or with a different ending, they could be interested.

A word of warning – publishing is a fluid industry. People are constantly moving between publishing houses and agencies, starting new companies, or combining with others.

Usually, the agent or publisher has a reputation for a certain genre, so even if they go to a different company, they'll probably still handle the same kind of writing. If you have a relationship with someone, that might continue through their job change.

28. Wait again.

An agent has a reputation, including the genre they handle, the quality of their authors' writing, and the publishers who sign their authors. If that reputation is a good one, they probably have more than enough successful authors in their roster.

However, an agent who is looking for clients isn't necessarily unsuccessful. With books in development, production, or already on the market, they may have plenty of time to pitch other books and actively seek new authors.

You may ask, "Why do I need an agent?"

Agents are the first step in sifting through submissions. They will normally only accept clients whose work is well-written and follows the rules of grammar and good writing.

Publishers know this, so an agented manuscript has already passed one gateway.

Some publishers will ONLY accept submissions from an agent. That doesn't mean that they'll offer a contract if you have an agent, just that they're more likely to read your query or proposal.

There is no guarantee that you'll get an agent, no matter how long you wait. For one thing, writers out-number agents. Each agent can represent dozens of authors and at any given moment, can be reading submissions, pitching to publishers, and receiving royalties on successful books. All of this takes time, so it's best to just wait.

Be polite when contacting agents and let them go if they're not interested. Remember, this is a relationship business and you don't want to burn any bridges.

You wouldn't want to marry someone who had to be talked into it. They wouldn't be committed to the relationship.

So wait for the right one.

29. When an agent wants to represent you, they'll send a contract.

A pitch to an agent consists of your query or proposal, including samples of your writing. The agent wants to know that you're a good writer and can create a product that he or she likes. And they need to know that your book will sell as well.

If an agent decides to represent you, they'll send a contract. It may be for just this book, for a series if that's what you proposed, or until either of you cancels the contract. My agent's contract is the last option – Steve Hutson will represent me and all my books until one of us decides to end the relationship.

Your agent will work for free until your first book starts to sell. All the editing, feedback, pitching, and negotiating your agent does cost you nothing. Do NOT pay an agent a cent.

If an agent asks for money up front, run away as fast as you can. And if he asks you to fix your manuscript, take that suggestion. He wants your product to be the best it can be so he'll be proud to sell it.

Your contract will state how much of your royalties will go to your agent. The amount can range from 10% up. But when you think of all the time the agent is putting in, selling your manuscript while you're writing your next book instead of having to pitch to publishers, it's well worth it.

Read the entire contract. You may want to get legal advice on it, because it is a binding agreement. Be sure there's a way for you to cancel the contract if necessary. Not that you want to, but just in case.

If your agent gets you a book contract, he or she is entitled to all royalties for that book, even if your contract with the agent is later cancelled. It's only fair, after all, since they did all that work up front.

30. Be nice to your agent.

Your agent will now be the one reading your rejection letters instead of you. Treat them like a respected friend. They'll do all the submitting, waiting, receiving rejections, and being ignored, so your self-esteem can remain intact.

Without an agent, you receive all the rejections or "ignores" from your submissions. That can be difficult to handle. Imagine having 60 first dates and never getting to Date Number 2. Eventually, you'd feel like you weren't meant to be in a relationship.

Your agent may let you know when he sends your proposal to a number of publishers. He might contact 15 or 20 and wait for responses. After a few months, he may have several rejections or have just been ignored. But you personally don't have to face all that negative feedback.

My agent, Steve Hutson, and I have a great relationship. I met him at a writers' conference and we had one 15-minute appointment. That's the only time I've seen him face-to-face. All our conversations now are on the phone, by email, or messages on Facebook. I don't mind how we communicate, as long as we do.

Steve appreciates that I'm flexible and not demanding. I've learned the process and know all that's involved, so I didn't expect him to get my book to market in six weeks. Because I was patient with him, he worked hard for me.

We now have an open-ended contract for the first book and look forward to working on other books as well.

You could have the same. Shop around until you find the right agent, then be nice to him or her.

31. Your agent might be working on a deal.

I heard an agent talk about one particularly difficult client. This author expected to have a publishing contract within a few months of signing for representation. When that didn't happen, she contacted the agent, yelled at him for not doing a good job, and cancelled her contract.

What she didn't know was that he was negotiating a three-book deal for her, but he wasn't at liberty to discuss it until the publisher's offer was in writing. When she blew up, she blew it.

The potential contract went away with the agent, and the author was back to square one. Unfortunately, when she pitched to the same publishers, they weren't interested. Her reputation sabotaged her possible success.

Patience is not only a virtue; it's crucial. Nothing happens fast in publishing, and being impatient doesn't help. After all, your book wasn't written in a week, so don't expect the other steps to be done that fast either. Movies would have you believe otherwise, but it takes a lot of time.

If you're concerned that your agent isn't representing you properly, call and talk with him. Treat him like a friend who's doing you a favor. Remember, he's working for free until your book comes out, so basically he's volunteering his time for you. Let him know you appreciate that.

My proposal was for the first of a series, and I listed other titles. As a result, my agent's contract is for every book I write until I cancel the contract. And my publisher's contract is open-ended as well. I can get published as long as I keep writing and maintain the relationships.

You can get the same. Just realize that you're working with flesh-and-blood people, and treat them the way you want to be treated.

32. Wait some more.

It takes months, sometimes years, to receive an acceptance and a contract from a publisher. And then months or years to get it in print.

If you want a book published, you spend a lot of time waiting. I know this is getting old, but it's true.

Most publishers want their authors to write at least three books, not just one. They're looking for a relationship with you, not just a one-time fling. In fact, if you mention a series in your proposal, you increase the chance of a contract. Once you develop an audience, you're more likely to be able to sell your second and third books to them.

This doesn't mean that you sit and twiddle your thumbs while you wait. Think of it like baking a cake. You work on the cake until the pan goes into the oven. But you don't have to sit and watch it bake. Go do something else.

You have another book inside of you, wanting to get out. So get at it. Maybe by the time you get a contract for the first book, you could have the second manuscript ready to submit.

Engross yourself in the publishing industry by writing, reading, and learning all you can about the process. This can help you to become a better writer.

33. Consider self-publishing, AKA independent publishing.

Once upon a time, self-publishing was known as "vanity press." It was a way for not-so-good writers to pay a publisher to produce their books.

That reputation has disappeared as more bestsellers have been independently published. Some of those were later bought by publishing houses and traditionally published. Other authors decided that if they could sell thousands or millions of copies and keep all the royalties, they didn't need a publisher.

Traditionally, the publisher pays all production costs. But in self-publishing, the author pays the costs. With subsidy publishing, the costs are shared between publisher and author.

There are a variety of ways to self-publish. Some publishing houses want you to agree to buy a lot of books to cover production costs. That would involve a huge financial outlay on your part and boxes of books in your garage, waiting for you to sell them. I (and a lot of other first-time writers) made this mistake.

Instead, you could publish as Print On Demand (POD). Then, a copy is printed ONLY when someone orders it. This may lower your royalties and cost a little more per book, but there is less investment up front. And these are easier to bring to market.

Also consider publishing as an electronic book or eBook. E-publishing will give you a higher percentage of royalties, so that may be a wise choice.

There are lots of electronic formats, so you need to do even more research to decide where you want to market your book and what format your readers use. If you can figure out how to format your eBook, you'll have minimal setup costs. You may need or pay someone to do it, but formatting must follow strict guidelines, so do your homework.

Whether you choose POD, hard copy, or e-pub, you'll need an ISBN (International Standard Book Number) for each type of book. And a paper copy needs a bar code for bookstores. These will add to your initial costs.

ISBNs and bar codes are available from Bowker.com. If you'll be writing more than one book, check out quantity discounts. As of this printing, one ISBN costs $125.00 and 10 cost $275.00, just a little more than two purchased separately!

34. You will need to buy your own books.

This doesn't sound fair, but it's just the way it is. There are several reasons you will need to buy your book, even though you wrote it.

If you publish traditionally, your publisher has purchased your manuscript, or adopted your "baby." The book is no longer yours and they're under no obligation to give you anything other than the royalties agreed upon in your contract.

Usually, you will get the wholesale/bookstore discount of 40% or maybe a little more. Then, you can sell the books you've bought for the retail price printed on the jacket and keep the difference. That is usually a lot more than what you'd earn in royalties for those books sold online or in bookstores.

If you've self-published or subsidy published, the books are usually Print On Demand (POD). You purchase through your publisher for the actual cost of production.

As of this printing, that's about $5 or less per book. When you do public speaking and sell your books in the back of the room, you can retail them at a discount from the price printed on the back and still make a good profit.

At that low rate, you can afford to give them away as a sort of "business card" to someone who needs one, or maybe someone who represents a group you want to reach.

And it's a great incentive to give away a copy or two during your presentation to the group. When the recipients get excited about having a book, others may want one as well.

One friend self-published a book that cost her $4 a copy POD. She bought 100 books for $400 and sold them for $12 each. Her initial outlay was soon recovered by her sales and her profit of $800 went toward more books.

It goes without saying that the more books you sell, the more you'll make.

35. Don't hold out for an advance.

An "advance" is royalty money paid to an author prior to publication. That means that the publisher gives you some money in advance of the release date, before any books are sold.

When your book is released, your publisher will retain all the profits until your advance is covered, then you start to receive royalties. Your royalty statement will show the amount of any advance deducted before you start getting checks.

Let's look at some numbers to help understand this.

Say a traditional publisher pays you a $500 advance. Your royalties are about $1 for each book sold. Any statement you receive will have $0 paid to you until at least 500 books are purchased to cover the money you already got.

Then, you'll get a check for royalties on all books sold over 500.

By the way, royalties are usually paid twice a year. Some publishers might pay more often, but don't expect a check every two weeks. Also, some won't cut a check for less than $250, so you may get some statements with no payout.

Royalties for online sales are sometimes paid monthly, but only if you have automatic deposit to your bank or PayPal account. These payments have no minimum, so you don't have to earn $250 before you get paid.

These days, very few publishers offer any money up front. They want to be assured that you'll work on selling your own book, and if you have pocketed some cash, you may not have that incentive.

If you've received an advance and don't complete your obligations to get the book out, you may be liable to pay it all back. But if the publisher doesn't release the book for whatever reason, you do not have to repay the advance.

At any rate, don't insist on an advance. You may never get published.

36. Read a contract before you sign it.

This step should be obvious. You should read every contract before you sign, not just a publishing contract. There may be fine print that would be less than favorable for you.

The more contracts you read, the more familiar you'll become. If you've signed agreements for a car, satellite TV, or something else, go back and read them. When you understand the basics of a contract, you can better understand a new one.

I was fortunate enough to have held a job in corporate America negotiating contracts, so it's not a foreign language to me. But if you don't have that experience, you may want to consult an expert.

This is where an agent can be a great resource. Your agent is familiar with publishing contracts and knows what to look for and look out for. The contract will affect them as well, so they want it to protect both of you.

Be sure you're comfortable with the language in the contract. You can negotiate and ask that the wording be changed to make it more understandable. It's no good to have an agreement when you can't figure out what it is that you agreed to.

If you change anything on the contract, you must initial it to indicate that you approve and to let the publisher know of the change. This is standard legal procedure, but I wouldn't recommend changing much. They've used the same contract for other authors and may not want a custom agreement.

Never sign anything with unfilled blanks. Not that you shouldn't trust a publisher, but any blank spaces can be filled in after you've signed. That may commit you to something you don't want. Blanks that don't apply to your agreement can be filled in with N/A for Not Applicable.

Most publishers will send you two paper copies of a contract, with one original signed by them. Sign one copy and return it; keep the other for your records.

37. Research royalties offered and compare to the rest of the market.

Royalties are a percentage of the money made on books that is paid to authors. Normally, for traditional publishing, you'll earn about a dollar or less per book. And since most books sell fewer than 500 copies, you won't become rich on royalties.

Sometimes royalties are paid on retail price, but most times only on net profit. That means that your royalty will be a portion of the retail price MINUS the cost to print that book.

Here's an example: If it costs your publisher $4 to print a book that retails for $15, you get a percentage of the $11 difference, not of the full $15. At 10%, your royalty would be $1.10 per book.

Many times, the book will sell at a discounted price online and in bookstores, so your royalties would be reduced. If that same book sells for only $11, your royalty is a percentage of $7, or $.70 at the same rate.

Most royalties are between 10% and 20%. Some publishers will increase the percentage of your royalties with a quantity of books sold. You have to reach an exorbitant amount, say 25,000 books, but it's a goal to shoot for. This would be written into your contract, not negotiated later.

EBooks will usually have higher royalties, since there are no printing costs. These payouts can run 35% to 70%. Since eBooks are easier to bring to publication, it may be wise to publish your book electronically.

The price of your book should be about the same as your competition. If you overprice in order to earn more, no one will buy it. But if you underprice it, readers may think it's not a quality book.

Do your homework, create a good product, and the royalties will come.

38. Wait a little longer.

Publishers schedule production months or years in advance. A contract doesn't mean you'll be published immediately. Or ever.

When a traditional publisher buys your manuscript, it no longer belongs to you. They have full authority to make decisions about when, how, and even *if* it'll be published.

I have a friend who wrote a beautiful children's book. She went to a writers' conference and pitched to an agent who signed her and got her a traditional contract. The publisher paid a small advance.

My friend waited several years for her book to come out. The publisher kept delaying it, putting it on the back burner. Eventually, the publishing company decided they would no longer produce children's books, so this book wasn't published.

Fortunately, the author was polite through all this and continued to have a good relationship with her agent and the publisher. When this deal fell through, other publishers were interested in her writing and requested her next book.

The trick is to be patient. No secret here.

Just learn to let others do their jobs at their own pace and you do yours. Life is much easier that way.

If you can't wait for the normal process, read the step about self-publishing. You can get your book to market much sooner if you're willing to do a lot of the work yourself and pay for it.

39. Marketing is up to you, not the publisher.

Once upon a time, publishers would foot the bill and all an author had to do was write. Besides investing all the production costs, the publisher would pay for marketing, transporting the author to book signings and speaking engagements, and holding back royalties until they were making money.

Nowadays, a publisher is unwilling to invest in a book unless they are certain that the book will sell thousands of copies. That usually only happens for a bestselling author with a proven track record.

Learn all you can about how to market your book and yourself. Even if all your friends and family members buy a copy, you'll need to sell more. Unfortunately, not even all your friends and family members will buy one. Many will expect you to give them one free, but, as you know, the books are not free to you.

One author friend of mine was disappointed with her lack of sales. She commented, “I need to find more friends so I can get them to buy my book.” Even that wouldn’t guarantee that she’d sell more. And when her new friends do buy the book, what then? Find more?

Marketing is an ongoing process. It’s not a “Let’s launch the book and wait for the sales to come in” endeavor.

There are speakers who write and writers who speak. If you’re not a speaker, learn how to become one. Then, get booked for speaking engagements. You can sell your book in the back of the room, which will result in pocketing more profit than your royalties. It’s also a great way to get people talking about you and your book.

There are lots of free training classes on marketing and speaking, some webinars, some teleseminars, and some in person. Keep learning and marketing.

40. Send a copy of your book when you request an interview.

When someone considers interviewing you on their radio or TV show, they'll want to know as much about you and your book as possible. That may include reading your entire book, or at least perusing it.

When my publicist requested 125 copies of my book, I choked. What? 125 copies? Didn't he realize how much those cost me?

Yes, he did. And he also knew that a free book is a "calling card" for an author. If an author isn't willing to risk the cost of a book yet wants some free publicity from a radio or TV show, their chances of an interview are less.

In other words, if you're a serious author who expects to sell books as a result of this interview, you should foot the bill for one book plus shipping costs. If you don't believe in your book enough, no one else will believe in it either.

A quick word about shipping: Your book is considered to be MEDIA by the US Post Office. As such, it doesn't need to be mailed first-class or Parcel Post. Media Mail is much cheaper, so be sure to ask for it. Delivery may take a little longer, but it could be worth saving a few dollars.

You might want to write a personal note to the host or producer in the book and sign it before you send it. They'll appreciate the personalization and be more likely to hold onto the book than just toss it.

One international TV host loved my book so much, she insisted that we tape two half-hour shows instead of the one that was scheduled. She had highlighted and Post-it®'ed it so much, she almost read the whole book on-air!

It was well worth the cost of one book to me.

41. Hire a publicist.

There is a difference between a publisher and a publicist.

- A PUBLISHER will publish your book.
- A PUBLICIST will get publicity for you and your book.

Just like an agent or a publisher, a publicist will specialize and develop a reputation in one or a few genres. When you pitch or approach someone to set up your interviews for you, be sure they're known for your type of book.

Their reputation can help to get interviews where those you want to reach are listening or watching. This will work to your advantage, because your target audience will meet you and your book.

Your publicist will want to start publicity four to six months before your book is released. They will set up radio and TV interviews for you to create "buzz," people talking about you and your book.

Most interviews sound spontaneous and natural, but they're very structured and preplanned. Your publicist will create a list of questions and send them to the show's producer. He'll also send you the list so you can write out your answers and practice so your conversation sounds casual.

A publicist is hired for a short amount of time, usually a few months. Don't have a heart attack when you find out how much they charge, but research online and compare.

If you can find the name of a publicist for a bestselling author in your genre, they may be a good resource for you, since they have a reputation. But you'll pay for it – a lot.

Look on bookstore shelves for books that yours will be competing with. Try to find out who those authors use for a publicist and ask if they'd represent you as well. Hopefully those books were well-written so their audience can be yours too.

42. Practice being interviewed.

Some people have no problem speaking in public. Put a microphone in their hands, and they can talk for hours.

Most writers are not like that. We tend to be introverts, so appearing on a radio or TV show can be intimidating.

Though your publicist will give you the list of questions for interviewers to use, the answers won't "just come to you" during your on-air chat. Even when you're intimately familiar with your book and comfortable speaking, your mind can go blank.

Write your answers to all the questions. I even wrote down the page number in my book for each answer in case I wanted to read it verbatim. The questions were in black on a Word doc, so I typed my answers in blue. That way, they stood out so I wouldn't get lost trying to find what I wanted to say.

Before you go on-air, have a friend role-play with you. You could do this sitting at your kitchen table, pretending you're in studio with the host. Or you might do it over the phone. I'd recommend that you try it both ways, since you will likely have some of each.

The more you practice, the more relaxed you'll be. If you're too nervous, people will be more concerned with your nerves than your book.

Television appearances are almost always done in person. Start with local stations so you won't have travel costs. As you get better known, you could get booked on national shows and may have to travel at your own expense.

Most radio interviews are done by phone. If you're in the same city, drive to the studio. Hosts love to have guests, since much of what they do is over the phone or microphone. If it's too far, you may need to call or they'll call you. Most producers will tell you to use a hardwired land line, not a cell phone, for better transmission.

An interview is a way for people to get to know you. Relax and enjoy.

43. Find an image consultant.

An image consultant is an expert who helps you look good.

Some would have you believe this is a waste of time and money. But if you witnessed the Kennedy-Nixon debates, you know that John Kennedy won mainly because Richard Nixon had a serious five-o'clock shadow. He looked worse, and people didn't trust him. Of course we learned later ... but that's another story. The point here is that their looks made the difference.

That's what a good image consultant can do for you. They will suggest what colors to wear, what clothes look best on you, and what accessories will complement work best. Use this information for your daily attire, not just for interviews and speaking engagements.

The consultant will also provide tips for television appearances. You want to be credible, and looking the part can go a long way toward that.

I had an appointment with an image consultant as part of a marketing program. She checked out my website and some photos I emailed her. Then, since she was across the country, our consultation was by phone.

She told me what clothing colors look best for my skin and hair colors, how to change my makeup, and ways to improve my appearance. I implemented those suggestions, and even a waitress at lunch the next day commented on how good I looked.

Be open to suggestions, even if you think you could never wear that color or cut your hair like that.

You've looked at your face in a mirror for years. It's time to get an objective opinion from an expert.

44. Research your interviewer.

This one takes time, but it's well worth the effort.

If you regularly listen to a radio show, you know the host and a little bit about them – married or not, approximate age, experiences they've had. It's easy to have a conversation with them, because you're familiar.

However, when you're being interviewed, you might be talking with a virtual stranger in another city. All you get from your publicist is their name, nothing else. Your talk can be more personal if you have listened to their show, read their biography and know a little about them before your interview.

The easiest way is to check the radio or TV station's website. Make some notes to help you remember. And try to watch or listen to at least one show.

I was interviewed on radio by a nationally-known personality about my cancer book. My publicist had mentioned that this host had been treated for cancer, but I didn't write it down. When it came up during the interview, I sounded like I had never heard. What could have been a connection between us turned into an awkward moment.

You don't need to connect on social media with the host. In fact, they may think you're stalking them. Just learn what you can and let it color your conversation.

Think of it like internet dating. You learn some things about the other person and discuss them the first time you meet. Simple as that.

Treat your host like a friend. Relax and talk with them the way you would on their living room couch. It's not only less stressful, but it's also more fun for you and your audience. They'll be more apt to like you and want to buy your book. And that's the whole reason for the interview!

45. Let your contacts (your platform) know about any interviews you have.

Your publicist will notify you when you have an interview scheduled. And if you have a contact for a radio, TV, or news show, you can arrange interviews as well.

Most radio programs are streamed online so those in other cities and states can listen real-time. Others are recorded as podcasts and can be heard at the listener's convenience.

Post on social media and tell all your friends and contacts about any interview you have and how they can listen or watch. They can pass this info on to their friends, increasing your audience, which will please your host and get you invited back.

It would be even better if you had a call-in time and lined up some friends to call with questions or comments. Radio hosts love audience interaction.

A word of warning here – Remind your guests to call. After an initial interview on a local radio show about my first book, I became a regular guest. Two family members said they'd call in for one discussion, but forgot to listen. I had to share their stories second-hand. Both the host and I were disappointed.

But if you can get friends to call in, have them let their contacts know about their appearance on the show. That will increase the audience, your platform, and your book sales.

The more you talk, the more people will hear and tell others about you and your book.

46. Don't expect to be paid for being on TV or radio shows.

This may be disappointing, but no one pays you to be interviewed. These appearances are considered publicity or advertising for your book. You were invited because of your book, not because of your dazzling personality.

We've all seen celebrities being interviewed about a book they've written, a movie coming out, or a new TV show. They aren't getting paid, either. They know that if they can increase their readership, their box office, or their audience, they will benefit.

I once saw a major star get upset on an interview because he wasn't getting paid. He said it was just a five-minute "commercial" for his movie, got up, took off his mic, and walked off the set. As a result, few went to see the movie, it bombed, and I haven't seen him in a hit motion picture since.

If you must travel for an interview, you will likely have to foot the bill. Weigh the cost of travel against the audience you can reach to see if it would be worth the trip.

I once flew from Colorado to South Carolina for an early morning TV taping. I paid airfare, but the show covered ground travel, dinner, and one night in a hotel.

The show had an audience of over 200 million, which would increase my platform dramatically. Fortunately, the host liked my book so much that we taped two shows instead of just one. It was well worth my expense.

As you go farther on your publishing road, you can track differences connected to your interviews. After appearing on a particular show, you may see an upswing in book sales. And if it's on a local show, bookstores in or near that town may reorder more books as a result.

That's your pay for interviews – more royalties in your pocket. It's not immediate, but it's still money.

47. Write thank-you notes to the producer and the host.

A producer is the one who schedules every segment of the show and keeps the host on time for the next guest. The host is the person who actually interviews you.

After every appearance, write thank-you notes to both the host and the producer for letting you be on their show.

Sending personal notes by snail mail has become a thing of the past. It's so easy to type a quick "TY" and click Send. Good enough? Maybe. But that doesn't have a lasting effect.

A written thank-you note can end up on someone's desk or pinned on their wall. And that reminder next to their computer monitor just may get you another appearance. So few people bother with a note that you'll stand out from the crowd.

It's worth the investment to buy cards and mail them. Since they're a business expense, they're tax deductible. But even more important, they show that you're a real human, someone who cares and takes the time to be thankful.

When a host leaves a show, the producer usually stays. Stay on the good side of the producer and you could be invited back.

Remember the TV talk show, "Live with Regis and Kathie Lee"? Neither Regis nor Kathie Lee is still around, but Gelman, the producer, is.

If you have a good relationship with the producer, when your subject comes up or you contact him or her again, they'll remember and book you – often. Especially if you have established yourself as an expert on a particular subject.

48. Keep a detailed record of your appearances and contacts.

If you have a good publicist, you'll have dozens of radio and TV interviews. And you may have some book signings or personal appearances where you can talk and read sections of your book.

No matter how good your memory is, you will forget some of these. In order to keep track of where you've appeared and who you've spoken with, create a spreadsheet with their contact info and when and how (in person, call-in, etc.) you were on the show.

Add personal info about the host or producer, such as their hobbies or children's names, anything that comes up in conversation. Also note whether the talk went well or not.

This will come in handy when you schedule publicity for your next book. Check the spreadsheet for past appearances and connections you made. Go to their websites to verify that the contact information is still the same.

Then, when you request an interview, mention that you were on the show before and use that as a springboard. Tell them what the topic was then and what you'll talk about this time. Give them book titles so they can look them up, if necessary.

Chances are, if it was a good first interview, they'll remember and invite you back. If it wasn't so good, don't hold your breath. They may remember that as well. This is one reason you don't want to burn any bridges and want to always be polite and friendly.

Be sure your spreadsheet has columns for dates: when you were first on, when you asked to be on this time, when you revisited. You don't want to be a pest and accidentally send several requests to the same person. They'll remember that as well.

49. Don't quit your day job.

Only about 5% of writers can support themselves and their families on what they earn with their writing. It's like making it big in Hollywood: A few are lucky; the rest perform for the love of the craft.

Don't let this discourage you.

I have writer friends who work fulltime jobs and still manage to carve out two hours a day to write. They've published several books and are enjoying mild success. You can do it too. Just keep at it.

Most writers will publish only one book, maybe make a splash, and then fade into memory. If you're like Harper Lee, you could write another "To Kill a Mockingbird" as your only published book and live off the royalties for the rest of your life. (Well, she did publish the sequel 50 years later, but she's the exception.)

Most of us won't find critical acclaim and financial success from one book. Even the "instant success" of the "Left Behind" series, which sold over 200 million copies, came after co-authors Tim LaHaye and Jerry B. Jenkins had each published over a hundred books.

If you have a new idea, a heart-stopping story, or a different way of doing something, share it with the world. It may cost you a little bit to publish, but, if you're willing to work on selling it, you can recoup your initial outlay and maybe earn a little more.

You can also make money selling articles to magazines. In fact, this is a great way to advertise your book. At the end of most articles, you get to have a short bio and include info about your book. The article will help to grow your audience by getting them familiar with your name and your writing style.

Maybe you won't write a bestseller, but your book could make a difference in one person's life. That makes it all worth it.

50. Write every day.

Some people keep a journal, writing their experiences, thoughts, feelings, hopes, dreams, or whatever. They do this every night before they forget what happened to them that day.

You could do the same. End your day writing all the things in your brain. Or you can start the day and write while your mind is fresh.

Pick a time when your brain works best. Be flexible, since your schedule probably won't be the same every day.

I was always a morning person when I went to a day job. My first book was written mostly in the morning, sitting at my desk at home. Then I found myself writing on my couch, where I'm more comfortable and feel creative. Now, I do my best work late afternoon or evening.

Find a place, time, and environment where your brain can let go of all that's inside. And just write.

You don't need to stare at your monitor. Every once in a while, I get bogged down correcting my typos or formatting my work and lose my train of thought. That's when I use a piece of paper to cover my monitor and just type. I let the words flow without interruption for a few paragraphs, then go back and edit.

Set a goal for the amount of time you'll write each day. It might work better if you put it on your calendar.

Treat it as importantly as you'd treat a meeting at your job. After all, this is the work that only you can do – writing your book. If you consider this your job, you won't have trouble writing every day.

After all, a painter paints, a baker bakes, and a writer writes. So get writing! The world is waiting to read it.

Have at it!

Now you know the basics. Writing and publishing a book involves a very long and complicated process, but it's not impossible. Others have done it before you, and you can do it, too.

Begin writing today. And if you already started a book and gave up, go back to it.

The world is waiting to hear what you have to say. So say it!

Appendix 1

Helpful resources:

- *How to Write a Book Proposal* by Michael Larsen
- *Jumpstart Your Publishing Dreams: Insider Secrets to Skyrocket Your Success* by W. Terry Whalin
- *On Writing: a Memoir of the Craft* by Stephen King
- *Proofreading Secrets of Best-Selling Authors* by Kathy Ide, originally published as *Polishing the PUGS: Punctuation, Usage, Grammar and Spelling* – great resource for grammar
- *The Writer's Digest Guide to Query Letters* by Wendy Burt Thomas
- *Unleash the Writer Within* by Cecil Murphey
- Writer's Digest Magazine and www.WritersDigest.com. Both have lots of info.

- *Writing for the Soul: Instruction and Advice from an Extraordinary Writing Life* by Jerry B. Jenkins
- ISBNs and bar codes can be obtained from www.Bowker.com.

Endnotes

[1] www.goodreads.com/quotes
[2] Stephen King, *On Writing; A Memoir of the Craft* (Scribner, 2000) p. 222.
[3] Ibid. p. 276.

About the Author

In spite of life not going as planned, **Debbie Hardy, The Queen of Resilience**, maintains a positive outlook and a joyful personality. She has overcome a childhood of poverty and abuse, a failed marriage, widowhood, and many other disappointments to become CEO (Chief Encouragement Officer) of Stepping Through Life.

- Debbie is the author of ***Stepping Through Cancer: A Guide for the Journey***, a resource for cancer caregivers. The American Cancer Society often requests copies of her book for their Relays for Life
- The first in a series of books, ***Free to Be Fabulous: 100 Ways to Look and Feel Younger at 40, 50, and Beyond***, was released in 2015.

- The next Fabulous book will be ***Free to Be Fabulous at Christmas: 100 Ways to Celebrate Without a Credit Card.*** Others will be about being fabulous at work, fabulous after divorce, and fabulous as a widow.

Debbie has appeared on local, national and international radio and TV shows. She also speaks to various groups and associations, including women's gatherings, retreats, professional caregivers, and Relays for Life with the American Cancer Society. Debbie teaches at writers' conferences and mentors other writers and authors.

In her spare time, she writes devotions and magazine articles, contributes to anthologies, plays the piano, and is a really cool grandmother.

Check out her website at www.DebbieHardy.com.